Ankita Rossi

Mosel Radweg
(Moselle Cycle Path)

Title: Mosel Radweg (Moselle Cycle Path)
Author: Ankita Rossi
Published by: NEXTUNICORN PUBLISHER PROPRIETORSHIP
Publisher's Address: Shree Dwarkadhish Ji Ka Was, Emri, Rajsamand, RAJASTHAN, India. Pincode: 313342
Printer Details: Published online on various platforms.
Edition: 01
ISBN: 978-81-968306-5-6

Images Source: Pixbay: (https://pixabay.com/)

Disclaimer: The author and publisher disclaim all liability for accuracy, loss, or damage arising from the use of this travel guide; users are urged to independently verify information and prioritize personal safety.

Catalog

Welcome to Mosel Radweg

Welcome to the Mosel Radweg, where you'll embark on a captivating journey filled with cultural treasures. This scenic route, with stops like Trier, Bernkastel-Kues, and Cochem, is a testament to the region's rich history and charm. While Paris may have its own allure, the Mosel Radweg stands out with its enchanting destinations that reveal the Roman past and medieval wonders that have shaped this beautiful pathway.

Let's start in Trier, a city nestled along the Mosel River that unveils ancient Roman relics such as the Porta Nigra and the Amphitheater. The cathedral and Electoral Palace showcase the city's architectural prowess while echoing tales of emperors and bygone eras.

Next stop is Bernkastel-Kues, where you'll be transported back in time to experience medieval splendor. The timber-framed houses and iconic Michael's Fountain bring the medieval ambiance to life. Don't miss exploring the bustling medieval market square and centuries-old vineyards that contribute to the region's renowned wines.

Cochem awaits with its fairytale-like Reichsburg Castle towering over the Mosel River. Immerse yourself in the historic charm of Cochem's Old Town with its half-timbered houses and cobblestone streets that tell stories of yesteryears.

As you pedal along the Mosel Radweg, you'll be accompanied by tales of centuries past woven by the river itself. Quaint villages dotting your path each have their own unique charm and story waiting to be discovered. Take your time exploring local artisans' craftsmanship, learning about winemaking traditions, and experiencing firsthand the welcoming spirit of this enchanting region.

Prepare your taste buds for a gastronomic adventure as you indulge in flavors unique to Mosel cuisine. From hearty regional dishes like Saumagen (stuffed pig's stomach) to delicate desserts like Quetschekuche (plum cake), every bite is a celebration of local ingredients and time-honored recipes.

Of course, no visit to the Mosel region is complete without experiencing its world-class wines. Traverse the vineyard-covered hills, visit family-owned wineries, and savor the nuances of Riesling, the region's flagship grape. From crisp and mineral to lusciously sweet, each sip will take you on a journey through the terroir.

Beyond the cultural gems lies the breathtaking natural landscapes of the Mosel Radweg. Pedal through hills covered in vineyards, witness the serenity of the Mosel River, and be captivated by lush greenery that frames your path. Whether exploring Eifel National Park or taking a leisurely ride through Hunsrück, you'll find a harmonious blend of adventure and tranquility in these picturesque landscapes.

1. Trier:

Let's dive into the fascinating history of Trier, which was established by the Celts in the late 4th century BC and later became a prominent Roman imperial residence. It holds the distinction of being Germany's oldest city.

One of the key attractions in Trier is the impressive Porta Nigra, an ancient Roman city gate that stands as a testament to its rich history. The Amphitheater and Electoral Palace are also worth exploring, showcasing a beautiful blend of Roman and Baroque architecture.

To make the most of your visit, it's recommended to plan your trip during spring or early autumn when the weather is more mild and pleasant.

If you're interested in visiting Porta Nigra, keep in mind that it is generally open daily, but it's always a good idea to check their official website for specific opening hours.

For any inquiries or further information, you can contact them at +49 651 978080 or visit their official website: [Official Website](https://www.trier-info.de/en)

And here's a hidden gem that you wouldn't want to miss - The Karl Marx House! This historical site holds special significance as it is where the renowned philosopher was born. It offers a unique glimpse into his life and ideas.

2. Bernkastel-Kues:

Dating all the way back to 1291, the town has managed to maintain its medieval charm and character in an impressive manner. One of the main highlights of this place are its timber-framed houses, Michael's Fountain, and the bustling market square. If you're wondering when is the best time to pay a visit, September is highly recommended, especially during the Bernkasteler Doctor Wine Festival. The market square and other outdoor attractions are open all year round for visitors to enjoy. For any inquiries or more information, you can contact them at +49 6531 500190 or check out their official website [here](https://www.bernkastel.de/en/). And of course, don't forget to indulge in the exquisite Bernkasteler Doctor wine that this place is famous for - it's truly a culinary delight!

3. Cochem:

Cochem boasts a rich history that can be traced all the way back to Roman times. One of its main attractions is the magnificent Reichsburg Castle, which was constructed in the 12th century. As you wander through the charming cobblestone streets of the Old Town, you'll be captivated by its beauty. Don't forget to take in the picturesque views of the Mosel River as well. The best time to visit Cochem is from May to September when the weather is pleasant. If you're planning a visit to Reichsburg Castle, make sure to check their official website for guided tour schedules. For any inquiries or further information, you can contact them at +49 2671 60040 or visit their [Official Website](https://www.burg-cochem.de/en/). As you explore this enchanting town, don't miss out on discovering one of its hidden gems - the Enderttor, one of the few remaining medieval gates that still exist today.

Koblenz, a city with a rich historical background, holds its roots as a Roman military post dating back over 2,000 years. Its historical significance is truly remarkable.

One of the main attractions in Koblenz is the Deutsches Eck, where the Mosel and Rhine rivers meet. This scenic spot is definitely worth a visit. Another must-see is the Ehrenbreitstein Fortress, which adds to the charm and allure of Koblenz.

To make the most of your trip, it's recommended to visit Koblenz during late spring to early autumn when the weather is pleasant and enjoyable.

If you plan on visiting the Ehrenbreitstein Fortress, rest assured that it's open year-round for visitors. For specific opening hours, it's advisable to check their official website for accurate information.

For any inquiries or further information, you can reach out to them at +49 261 19433 or visit their [Official Website](https://www.koblenz-touristik.de/).

When it comes to culinary delights in Koblenz, you must try "Koblenzer Sauerbraten," a local specialty that will tantalize your taste buds. It's an experience not to be missed!

5. Traben-Trarbach:

Traben-Trarbach, a town that flourished during the 19th and early 20th centuries due to its wine trade, offers a fascinating history. Its key attractions include the mesmerizing Art Nouveau architecture, enchanting underground wine cellars, and the picturesque Mosel River. To make the most of your visit, it is recommended to plan it during spring or summer when the weather is pleasant and wine festivals are in full swing. Keep in mind that opening hours for cellars may vary, so it's best to inquire locally for accurate information. If you're looking for a hidden gem in this wine-centric town, don't miss out on exploring the unexpected treasure of the Buddha Museum. For more details and contact information, you can reach out at +49 6541 83980 or visit their official website (https://www.traben-trarbach.de/en/).

6. Beilstein:

Let's delve into the fascinating history of a medieval village that has its roots dating all the way back to the 9th century. This charming wine village offers a delightful experience with its captivating Castle Metternich and breathtaking panoramic views of the Mosel region.

To make the most of your visit, it is recommended to plan your trip during the summer season. This is when you can enjoy pleasant strolls through the village and engage in various outdoor activities.

If you're interested in exploring Castle Metternich, do note that it has specific visiting hours. It's always a good idea to check locally for the latest information.

For any inquiries or further details, you can reach out at +49 2673 1332 or visit their official website [here](https://www.beilstein-mosel.com/).

When it comes to culinary delights, be sure to indulge yourself in the exquisite regional wines and savor the flavors of local Mosel cuisine at one of the traditional wine taverns available in this enchanting village.

Neumagen-Dhron, known as the oldest wine town in Germany, boasts a fascinating history rooted in its Roman heritage. One of its notable attractions is a replica of an ancient Roman wine ship, which adds to the charm of this picturesque destination. The peaceful landscapes along the Mosel river and the enchanting vineyards further enhance the appeal of Neumagen-Dhron. For those seeking an immersive experience, autumn is the best time to visit when the grape harvest creates a vibrant atmosphere. The Roman wine ship can be viewed throughout the year, allowing visitors to explore this unique piece of history at their convenience. To get in touch or gather more information, you can contact +49 6535 947327 or visit their official website at [Official Website](https://www.neumagen-dhron.de/en/). In addition to these well-known attractions, St. Dionysius Church stands out as a hidden gem with its remarkable Romanesque architecture and a distinctive apse that adds to its allure. Neumagen-Dhron offers a delightful blend of history and natural beauty that will captivate any traveler's heart.

8. Piesport:

Piesport, a place with a rich history dating back to Roman times, is widely acclaimed for its magnificent Goldtröpfchen vineyard. This charming destination offers several key attractions, including the Roman Wine Press, breathtaking vineyard panoramas, and of course, the renowned Goldtröpfchen vineyard itself. For those planning a visit, autumn is the ideal time to immerse yourself in the vibrant atmosphere of wine festivals. Do check locally for specific opening hours of vineyard tours and wine tastings. To get in touch with Piesport's treasures, you can contact them at +49 6507 2025 or explore their official website for more information (https://www.piesport.de/). While you're there, don't miss out on the opportunity to indulge in the culinary delights this region has to offer - from savoring local Riesling wines to treating your taste buds with delectable regional Mosel dishes.

9. Eltz Castle:

If we delve into the past, we come across the remarkable Eltz Castle, which was constructed back in the 12th century. This medieval treasure is tucked away in the hills, waiting to be discovered.

One of its captivating features is the majestic castle itself, enveloped by lush greenery. It truly stands as a sight to behold.

For those planning a visit, it is advisable to plan your trip between May and October. During this time, you can enjoy castle tours and bask in pleasant weather conditions.

To ensure you make the most of your visit, it's recommended to check the official website of Eltz Castle for guided tour schedules. This way, you can plan your day accordingly and not miss out on any fascinating insights.

If you wish to get in touch with Eltz Castle directly, you can reach them at +49 2672 95050 or visit their [Official Website](https://www.eltz.de/en/). They will be more than happy to assist you with any inquiries or concerns.

While exploring this hidden gem, don't forget about the enchanting Eltz Forest that surrounds it. The forest offers a plethora of hiking trails for nature enthusiasts and adventurers alike. It's an opportunity to immerse yourself in nature's embrace and create unforgettable memories.

10. Saarburg:

Saarburg, a town with a rich medieval history, was established way back in the 10th century. When it comes to attractions, this picturesque town has it all - from an impressive waterfall to stunning medieval architecture and even an old mill. If you're planning a visit, the best time to go would be during the summer when you can enjoy outdoor activities and also catch the annual Altstadtfest. The good news is that the waterfall and other outdoor attractions are accessible throughout the year. For any inquiries or further information, you can contact them at +49 6581 99410 or visit their official website at [Official Website](https://www.saarburg.de/en/). And of course, no trip to Saarburg would be complete without trying their renowned

"Saarweine" which you can find in local taverns. So make sure to indulge your taste buds while exploring this charming town!

11. Bremm:

Bremm has a rich history that is closely tied to the art of winemaking. Notably, it is home to the Calmont, which holds the title of being Europe's steepest vineyard. A visit to Bremm would not be complete without exploring this key attraction, as it offers breathtaking panoramic vistas of the Mosel. Late spring is considered the best time to experience pleasant weather and witness the blooming vineyards in all their glory. The Calmont is accessible for hiking at any time that suits you. For more information or inquiries, you can contact +49 6542 90100 or visit their official website at [Official Website](https://www.bremm-mosel.de/en/). Additionally, a hidden gem worth exploring in

Bremm is the St. Lawrence Church, a charming small village church that holds its own unique charm and beauty.

12. Alken:

Alken has a rich history that is closely connected with the medieval Burg Thurant, which was constructed in the 12th century. One of the main attractions in this charming Mosel town is the captivating Burg Thurant, where visitors can appreciate its medieval architecture and enjoy the delightful local wines. For those planning a visit, spring or summer would be an ideal time to explore Alken and take part in vineyard tours while enjoying pleasant weather. It's important to note that Burg Thurant has specific visiting hours, so it's recommended to check locally for more information. If you have any inquiries or need further details, you can contact them at +49 2605 3633 or visit their official website at [Official Website](https://www.alken-mosel.de/). Additionally, don't miss the opportunity to indulge in the culinary delights of Alken by trying out the local Riesling wines paired with regional Mosel specialties.

13. Ellenz-Poltersdorf:

Let me take you on a journey through time as we stroll along the narrow streets of this charming Mosel village. Feel the warmth and history that seeps through every corner, as these roots date back centuries.

As we explore the quaint village streets, you'll be immersed in the historic ambiance that surrounds you. It's like stepping into a different era, where every cobblestone tells a story.

To truly experience the magic of this place, I recommend visiting during autumn. This is when the grape harvest takes place and village festivals come alive with vibrant energy. It's an opportunity to witness traditions that have been passed down for generations. When it comes to opening hours, there are none! You can enjoy the village charm at your own leisure, taking your time to soak in every detail and embrace the slower pace of life.

If you need any information or have any questions, feel free to contact us at +49 2673 259. You can also visit our official website for more details on what this enchanting village has to offer.

Now, let me share with you a hidden gem that will leave you breathless - the Nikolauskapelle. This charming chapel not only exudes beauty but also offers panoramic views that will take your breath away. It's a true testament to the rich history and natural wonders that surround this village.

So come and experience all of this firsthand - narrow streets filled with stories from centuries past, historic ambiance at every turn, and hidden gems waiting to be discovered.

Welcome! If you're planning to explore the Mosel Radweg, there are a few important things you should know. Let's dive in!

Firstly, let's talk about currency. Along the Mosel Radweg, the official currency is the Euro (€).

Next up, language. German is the official language along the Mosel Radweg. While English is spoken in tourist areas, knowing a few basic German phrases can really enhance your interactions with locals and make your travel experience even more enriching.

Now let's discuss seasons. Each season along the Mosel Radweg offers its own unique advantages:

- High Season (Jul–Aug): Expect crowds, especially in August. Prices may be higher during peak times.

- Shoulder Season (Apr–Jun & Sep–Oct): This is a great time for budget-conscious travelers. You can enjoy festivals, blooming flowers, and local produce.

- Low Season (Nov–Mar): During this time, you can save up to 30% on costs. Keep in mind that some attractions may be closed, but major cities still thrive with cultural events.

In case of emergencies along the Mosel Radweg, it's important to have some vital contact numbers handy:

- Ambulance: 112

- Police: 110

- Fire: 112

While cycling along the Mosel Radweg, you might find these websites useful:

-    [Mosel Radweg Official Website](https://www.mosel-radweg.de/)

- [German Railways (www.bahn.de)](https://www.bahn.de/en)

-    [Agritourism in Germany (www.urlaub-auf-dem-bauernhof.de)](https://www.urlaub-auf-dem-bauernhof.de/)

Let's talk about daily costs now. Your budget can vary depending on your preferences:

- Budget (Less than €100): If you're on a budget, you can find hostel beds for €15-30, budget hotel rooms for €50-110, and affordable local meals for €6-12.

- Midrange (€100–€250): For a midrange experience, you can opt for hotel rooms priced at €110-200 and enjoy meals at local restaurants ranging from €25 to €50.

- Top End (More than €250): If luxury is what you seek, indulge in hotel rooms ranging from €200 to €450 and fine dining experiences costing around €50-150 per person.

Opening hours can vary based on the season along the Mosel Radweg. Here are some general guidelines:

- Banks: Open from 8.30am–1.30pm and 3.30–4.30pm, Monday to Friday.

- Restaurants: Usually open from noon–2.30pm and 7.30–11pm or even midnight.

- Shops: Operating hours are typically from 9am–1pm and 4–8pm, Monday to Saturday.

Now let's talk about arriving in Mosel Radweg. Here are some major transportation options from airports to city centers:

- Frankfurt Airport: You have the option of taking direct trains or shuttles for convenient travel.

- Luxembourg Airport: Accessible by bus or taxi services.

- Frankfurt-Hahn Airport: Shuttle buses are available for transfers to nearby towns.

- Cologne Bonn Airport: Well-connected with trains and buses.

With all these essential details in mind, you're now well-prepared to explore the beautiful Mosel Radweg while immersing yourself in its scenic beauty and cultural treasures.

Are you ready for an amazing cycling adventure along the stunning Mosel Radweg? Get ready to explore picturesque towns and breathtaking landscapes over a span of two weeks.

Let's start our journey from Trier to Bernkastel-Kues, where you can immerse yourself in the rich history of Trier, with its Roman Porta Nigra and Amphitheater. As you pedal along the Mosel Radweg, you'll be captivated by the medieval charm of Bernkastel-Kues, known for its timber-framed houses and Michael's Fountain.

Next stop, Cochem to Koblenz! Prepare to be enchanted by Cochem's fairytale-like settings, with its Reichsburg Castle overlooking the Mosel. Continue your cycling adventure along the Mosel Radweg until you reach Koblenz, where the majestic Mosel and Rhine rivers meet. Don't forget to explore the iconic Deutsches Eck and the historic Ehrenbreitstein Fortress.

After a few days of exploring Cochem and Koblenz, it's time to head towards Traben-Trarbach to Beilstein. Take a moment to relax in Traben-Trarbach's Art Nouveau architecture and discover its impressive underground wine cellars. Keep pedaling until you reach Beilstein, a charming wine village boasting a medieval castle that offers panoramic views of the Mosel.

Now let's cycle towards Neumagen-Dhron to Piesport! Neumagen-Dhron is known as Germany's oldest wine town, so make sure to explore its ancient Roman wine ship replica and enjoy the serene beauty of the Mosel landscapes. Finally, head towards Piesport where you can visit the Roman Wine Press and indulge in scenic vineyard panoramas from the famous Goldtröpfchen vineyard.

For our last leg of this incredible journey, let's take a short detour to Eltz Castle, a medieval gem nestled in the hills. After exploring the castle, continue cycling until you reach Saarburg, a picturesque town along the Saar River. Don't miss out on the impressive waterfall and medieval architecture that make Saarburg truly special.

Now, let's switch gears and dive into a culinary and cultural adventure along the Mosel Radweg for one week. Get ready to tantalize your taste buds with local flavors and discover historical gems.

Starting in Alken, take some time to admire the medieval Burg Thurant and indulge in some delicious local wines. Continue your journey to Ellenz-Poltersdorf, a traditional Mosel village with narrow streets and a warm ambiance. Make sure to explore the village and pay a visit to Nikolauskapelle, a charming chapel offering breathtaking panoramic views.

Next up is Neef to Maring-Noviand! Neef is a riverside town that exudes medieval charm dating back to the 8th century. Stroll through its historic streets and visit St. Johannis Church for an extra touch of history. Then cycle onwards to Maring-Noviand, renowned for its wine-making history that dates all the way back to Roman times. Take your time wandering through vineyards and don't miss out on visiting St. Mary's Church.

Our final destination for this culinary journey is Zell to Moselkern! Zell has deep-rooted winemaking traditions that trace back centuries ago during Roman times. Take a leisurely stroll along the Mosel promenade and soak in the relaxed atmosphere of this charming town before concluding your gastronomic adventure in Moselkern.

These thoughtfully crafted itineraries promise an unforgettable cycling experience along the Mosel Radweg where you'll be surrounded by natural beauty, cultural exploration opportunities, and mouthwatering culinary delights at every turn of your pedals.

The Mosel Radweg, also known as the Moselle Cycle Path, takes you on a captivating journey along the banks of the Moselle River. This scenic route offers a perfect blend of natural beauty and cultural heritage, making it a haven for cyclists and explorers alike. The history of this path runs deep, with roots that stretch back to ancient times.

Let's travel back in time to when the Moselle Valley was inhabited by Celtic tribes. The Romans saw the potential of the Moselle River for trade and military purposes and established settlements and fortifications along its shores. Even today, we can witness remnants of their influence through archaeological sites like the Roman bridge in Trier and the majestic Porta Nigra.

As we enter the medieval era, we see how the Moselle Valley became a hub for trade, particularly in wine. The steep hillsides were carefully terraced for vine cultivation, shaping the landscape as we know it today. Medieval towns such as Bernkastel-Kues and Cochem emerged as bustling centers of commerce, while the Moselle River facilitated transportation of goods, especially their renowned local wines.

The Renaissance brought about a cultural and economic revival along the Moselle. Princes and nobility invested in constructing splendid castles overlooking the river, like Burg Eltz which has become an icon. This period witnessed an upswing in wine trade with expanding vineyards that became an integral part of the region's identity.

Unfortunately, various wars disrupted the tranquility of this picturesque valley throughout history. The Thirty Years' War and Napoleonic Wars took their toll on castles, towns, and vineyards that bore witness to these conflicts' ravages. Today we can still see scars from those turbulent times at certain historical sites.

In post-World War II Europe's reconstruction phase came an increasing interest in visiting places like Moselle Valley for respite and cultural enrichment. It was during this time that the idea of the Mosel Radweg as a cycling route began to take shape. The aim was to showcase the region's beauty and history, creating an immersive experience for cyclists that weaves through the heart of the Moselle's past.

As interest in cycling grew in the late 20th century, efforts were made to develop the infrastructure of the Mosel Radweg. Dedicated cycling paths were created, and signage was carefully implemented to ensure a safe and enjoyable experience for cyclists of all levels. This transformation turned the Moselle Valley into a premier cycling destination.

Alongside infrastructure development, there was also a growing awareness of preserving the cultural heritage of this remarkable region. Conservation initiatives were put into action to safeguard historical sites, medieval castles, and vineyards. The Mosel Radweg became more than just a cycling route; it became a cultural corridor where travelers could immerse themselves in rich history while marveling at breathtaking landscapes.

The establishment of the Mosel Radweg had a positive impact on local communities along its route. Tourism flourished, bringing economic opportunities for small businesses, hotels, and local artisans. The revitalization of historical sites fueled by increased visitor traffic also fostered a renewed sense of pride and connection among the local population.

Contemporary Significance and Global Appeal:

The Mosel Radweg is a remarkable example of how history, nature, and recreation can come together harmoniously. It attracts cyclists from all corners of the world who are captivated by the charm of this scenic route. They eagerly pedal through slopes covered in vineyards, medieval towns, and alongside a river steeped in centuries-old stories. The Mosel Radweg has become a symbol of sustainable tourism, offering an environmentally friendly way to explore the region's cultural and natural wonders.

Cultural Festivals and Events:

The cultural revival along the Moselle is beautifully showcased through the multitude of festivals and events that take place along the Mosel Radweg. From wine festivals in Bernkastel-Kues to medieval fairs in Cochem, these gatherings have become an integral part of the region's identity. They not only highlight the liveliness of the Moselle Valley but also foster a sense of community among both locals and visitors.

Sustainable Tourism and Conservation Efforts:

As the popularity of the Mosel Radweg continues to soar, there is a growing focus on sustainable tourism practices. Conservation initiatives aim to strike a balance between welcoming visitors and preserving the delicate ecosystem as well as historical sites. Local communities actively participate in initiatives that promote responsible tourism, ensuring that future generations can also revel in the splendors offered by the Moselle Valley.

Conclusion:

In essence, the history of the Mosel Radweg weaves together threads from ancient civilizations, medieval prosperity, wartime challenges, and present-day endeavors towards preservation and sustainability. It transcends being just a cycling route; it stands as a living testament to both resilience and beauty found within every corner of this enchanting valley. All those who journey along its paths are invited to become partakers in its ongoing story.

Embarking on a cycling adventure along the Mosel Radweg opens up a whole new world of diverse accommodations, ensuring that every traveler can find the perfect haven to rest and recharge. Let me take you through a detailed guide to the various lodging options along the Mosel Radweg, including their approximate price ranges.

1. Historic Gasthofs:

As you journey along the Mosel Radweg, you'll come across historic gasthofs, which are traditional German inns known for their warm hospitality and local charm. These establishments truly capture the unique character of the region and provide a glimpse into its rich cultural heritage. Prices range from €60 to €120 per night.

2. Charming Guesthouses:

If you're looking for a more intimate and personalized experience, charming guesthouses are scattered along the route. Adorned with flower-filled balconies and nestled in picturesque villages, these guesthouses offer a serene atmosphere where you can fully immerse yourself in the local lifestyle. Prices range from €50 to €100 per night.

3. Riverside Retreats:

Imagine waking up to breathtaking panoramic views of the winding Moselle River - that's what riverside retreats along the

Mosel Radweg offer cyclists. Not only do they provide comfortable accommodation, but they also allow you to bask in the beauty of nature that surrounds you. Prices range from €70 to €150 per night.

4. Countryside Bed and Breakfasts:

Tucked away amidst rolling hills and vineyard-covered landscapes, countryside bed and breakfasts provide an authentic escape from everyday life. Here, you can enjoy peaceful tranquility while experiencing warm hospitality from your hosts in the charming Mosel Valley. Prices range from €40 to €90 per night.

5. Boutique Winery Stays:

For wine enthusiasts, boutique stays at local wineries offer a truly elevated experience. These accommodations not only provide tastefully decorated rooms but also offer wine tastings and the opportunity to learn about the rich winemaking traditions of the Moselle region. Prices range from €80 to €150 per night.

6. Castle Hotels:

If you have a passion for history and grandeur, the Mosel Radweg presents castle hotels along its course. Here, cyclists can indulge in a regal experience by spending the night within the walls of a medieval castle while still enjoying modern amenities. Prices range from €100 to €300 per night.

7. Quaint Farm Stays:

Embracing the rustic charm of the Mosel Valley, farm stays provide a unique blend of comfort and simplicity. Travelers can reconnect with nature, waking up to the delightful sounds of farm animals and savoring locally sourced produce. Prices range from €50 to €100 per night.

8. Modern Wellness Resorts:

Along certain segments of the Mosel Radweg, you'll come across areas known for their spa and wellness offerings. Cyclists seeking a touch of luxury can choose modern wellness resorts where they can indulge in rejuvenating spa treatments amidst breathtaking natural landscapes. Prices range from €120 to €250 per night.

9. Rural Holiday Apartments:

For those desiring a home-away-from-home experience, rural holiday apartments are an excellent choice. These self-contained units are often located in charming village settings and offer greater flexibility, making them perfect for extended stays along your cycling journey. Prices range from €60 to €120 per night.

10. Barge Hotels: Along the picturesque riverbanks, you can discover barge hotels that offer a unique lodging experience. Combining the charm of river travel with the comfort of a hotel, these floating accommodations provide a delightful stay. Prices range from €80 to €150 per night.

11. Budget-Friendly Hostels: For those on a tight budget, there are hostels along the Mosel Radweg that offer dormitory-style accommodations. These hostels create a sociable atmosphere, allowing travelers to connect with fellow cyclists from around the world. Prices range from €20 to €40 per night.

12. Camping Spots: Nature enthusiasts can embrace adventure by camping along the Mosel Radweg. Designated camping spots with essential facilities invite cyclists to spend a night under the stars, surrounded by the tranquility of the Moselle landscape. Prices range from €10 to €20 per night.

13. Local Homestays: To immerse yourself in local culture and gain insights into daily life along the Mosel Radweg, you may consider staying in local homestays. Interacting with residents and perhaps sharing a meal with them offers an authentic cultural experience. Prices range from €30 to €70 per night.

14.Technology-Driven Stay Options: Embracing modern conveniences seamlessly into their surroundings, some accommodations along the Mosel Radweg provide technology-driven experiences for guests who appreciate innovation while enjoying picturesque views.The price ranges from 70€ - 120€

15.Educational Farm Experiences: Families visiting this region may find educational farm stays particularly appealing for their children.Children can enjoy interacting with animals while parents appreciate the scenic beauty of Moselle region.Price Range is between 40€ - 80€ per night.

16.Sustainable Eco-Lodges: As sustainability becomes a focal point in travel, eco-lodges along the Mosel Radweg cater to environmentally conscious cyclists. These accommodations follow eco-friendly practices contributing to the preservation of the pristine Moselle environment. Prices range from €60 to €120 per night.

17.Adventure-Centric Campsites: For thrill-seekers, adventure-centric campsites along the Mosel Radweg offer an adrenaline boost amid serene landscapes. In addition to camping facilities, these sites may provide activities such as kayaking, hiking trails, or even zip-lining. Prices range from €15 to €30 per night.

18.Pet-Friendly Options: Recognizing the special bond between cyclists and their furry companions, there are pet-friendly accommodations available along the Mosel Radweg. Travelers can find welcoming stays that cater to the needs of both two-legged and four-legged guests.Price Range is between 40€ - 90€ per night. In conclusion, whether you prefer the charm of a barge hotel or the budget-friendly atmosphere of a hostel, there is a wide range of accommodation options available along the Mosel Radweg to suit every traveler's preferences. So go ahead and plan your stay while enjoying all that this beautiful region has to offer!

When embarking on a cycling journey along the beautiful Mosel Radweg, it is important to not only immerse yourself in the scenic landscapes but also be well-informed about the visa and residency regulations. To help you navigate through these travel requirements, here is a comprehensive guide:

1. Visa Requirements for European Citizens:

 - European citizens who come from countries participating in the Schengen Treaty can enter the region of Mosel Radweg with a valid identity card or passport.

2. Visa Exemptions for Select Countries:

 - Travelers from specific non-EU countries, including Australia, Canada, Japan, New Zealand, and the USA (to name a few), may not require visas if their visit to Mosel Radweg is for tourist purposes and does not exceed 90 days.

 - It's important to note that visa exemptions may vary for those planning to travel to non-Schengen countries like the UK and Ireland.

3. Visas for Non-EU and Non-Schengen Nationals:

 - Non-EU and non-Schengen nationals who plan on cycling along the Mosel Radweg for more than 90 days or have purposes other than tourism (such as study or work) might need specific visas.

- To find out detailed visa requirements, it's advisable to visit the official website of the relevant consulate or embassy. Make sure to verify all information before planning your journey.

4. Residence and Work for EU Citizens:

  - EU citizens who are cycling along the Mosel Radweg do not require permits to live or work during their trip.

  - However, if their stay exceeds three months, EU citizens should register at the municipal registry office where they reside. Proof of financial means may be required.

5. Permanent Residence for Non-EU Foreign Citizens:

  - Non-EU foreign citizens who have completed five years of continuous legal residence along the Mosel Radweg may be eligible to apply for permanent residence status.

6. Permit to Stay ('Permesso di Soggiorno'):

  - Non-EU citizens who plan on staying at the same address along the Mosel Radweg for more than one week should obtain a 'permesso di soggiorno' from the local police station.

  - It's important to note that tourists staying in hotels along the Mosel Radweg are usually exempt from this requirement.

  - However, if you are planning an extended stay for study, work, or other purposes, obtaining a 'permesso di soggiorno' is essential. This can be done through the police, and specific documents may be required during the application process.

7. Study Visas:

- Non-EU citizens who intend to study at institutions along the Mosel Radweg must apply for study visas at their nearest consulates or embassies.

- Required documents often include proof of enrollment, fee payment, and financial means to support oneself during studies.

- Study visas are issued for the duration of enrollment and can be renewed based on meeting certain criteria.

Understanding these visa and residency requirements is crucial for ensuring a seamless and legally compliant cycling journey along the enchanting Mosel Radweg. Always refer to official sources for the latest information to ensure that your travel plans unfold smoothly.

Detailed Route Descriptions for the Mosel Radweg

Embarking on the Mosel Radweg is like embarking on a journey filled with picturesque landscapes, charming towns, and rich history. The route winds along the Mosel River, taking you through vineyards and past historic landmarks. Let's dive into the detailed route descriptions, divided into manageable sections, each offering a unique blend of natural beauty and cultural richness.

Section 1: Trier to Bernkastel-Kues

- Distance: Approximately 50 km

- Key Landmarks:

  - Start your adventure in Trier, which happens to be Germany's oldest city. Take some time to explore the impressive Porta Nigra and the Roman Amphitheatre.

  - As you cycle along the river, you'll pass through delightful villages like Schweich and Mehring.

  - Finally, reach Bernkastel-Kues, a place known for its incredibly well-preserved medieval architecture and the iconic Michael Castle.

- Scenic Highlights:

  - Prepare to be mesmerized by vineyard-covered hillsides and the tranquil beauty of the Mosel River.

  - You'll also come across charming wine villages with their adorable half-timbered houses.

- Difficulty Rating:

 - This section is relatively easy to moderate in terms of difficulty since it mostly consists of flat terrain.

Section 2: Bernkastel-Kues to Cochem

- Distance: Approximately 60 km

- Key Landmarks:

 - Leave Bernkastel-Kues behind as you venture deeper into the heart of the Mosel wine region.

 - Along your way, you'll pass through Traben-Trarbach, famous for its stunning art nouveau architecture.

 - Your final destination is Cochem, dominated by the magnificent Reichsburg Castle.

- Scenic Highlights:

 - Get ready for breathtaking views as you cycle alongside meandering rivers adorned with countless vineyards.

 - The hills come alive with enchanting castles, perched on their slopes.

- Difficulty Rating:

 - This section is mostly flat with a few moderate ascents, making it suitable for cyclists of various skill levels.

Section 3: Cochem to Koblenz

- Distance: Approximately 50 km

- Key Landmarks:

 - Start your journey in Cochem and make sure to visit the impressive Reichsburg Castle.

- As you pedal away, you'll encounter charming towns like Beilstein and Zell.

- Your final stop is Koblenz, where the Mosel River meets the mighty Rhine. Don't miss exploring the Deutsches Eck and Ehrenbreitstein Fortress.

- Scenic Highlights:

- Vineyards and river panoramas will keep you company throughout this section.

- The riverside villages boast quaint timber-framed houses that add to the charm.

- Difficulty Rating:

- This section offers varied terrain, with some flat stretches and moderate ascents.

Section 4: Koblenz to Winningen

- Distance: Approximately 40 km

- Key Landmarks:

- Depart from Koblenz as you cycle through the picturesque Mosel Valley.

- Along your way, you'll pass by the charming town of Winningen, known for its historic architecture.

- Scenic Highlights:

- Enjoy a scenic ride along the riverside, surrounded by vineyards and orchards.

- Take in breathtaking views of the surrounding hills and valleys.

- Difficulty Rating:

- This section is generally flat and suitable for cyclists of all levels.

Section 5: Winningen to Trittenheim

- Distance: Approximately 30 km

- Key Landmarks:

   - Begin your adventure in Winningen as you pedal through stunning landscapes.

   - En route, you'll pass by Bernkastel-Kues with its medieval charm beckoning you to explore.

   - Finally, arrive in Trittenheim, a place embraced by vineyards.

- Scenic Highlights:

   - Enjoy the serene views of the Mosel River as you cycle along its banks.

   - Encounter historic towns and charming wine villages along the way.

- Difficulty Rating:

   - This section is mostly flat and suitable for cyclists of all levels.

These detailed route descriptions serve as a comprehensive guide for cyclists who wish to embark on the Mosel Radweg. Each section offers a delightful mix of cultural exploration and natural beauty, ensuring an unforgettable cycling experience along the Mosel River. So grab your bike, immerse yourself in the wonders of this route, and create memories that will last a lifetime!

The Mosel Radweg offers cyclists a delightful journey through enchanting landscapes and historic towns, made even easier with key junctions that guide their way. Let's explore these essential junctions along the route:

Junction 1: Trier's Porta Nigra

- Location: Trier

- Description: Embark on your Mosel Radweg adventure at the iconic Porta Nigra in Trier, a well-preserved Roman city gate. This junction not only marks the starting point but also introduces you to the rich history of Trier.

Junction 2: Schweich

- Location: Along the Mosel River

- Description: Pedal through the picturesque town of Schweich, where vineyards grace one side and the serene Mosel River flows on the other. This junction offers a delightful riverside route for cyclists to enjoy.

Junction 3: Bernkastel-Kues

- Location: Bernkastel-Kues

- Description: Immerse yourself in medieval charm as you reach Bernkastel-Kues. This junction beckons you to wander through cobbled streets, visit Michael Castle, and bask in the serene ambiance of the Mosel.

Junction 4: Traben-Trarbach

- Location: Traben-Trarbach

- Description: Known for its art nouveau architecture, this junction invites you to take a break and explore Traben-Trarbach. Marvel at impressive buildings that showcase the cultural heritage of this region.

Junction 5: Cochem and Reichsburg Castle

- Location: Cochem

- Description: Arrive in Cochem, where majestic Reichsburg Castle dominates the landscape. This junction serves as a gateway to medieval wonders, inviting you to tour the castle and delve into Cochem's rich history.

Junction 6: Koblenz - Deutsches Eck

- Location: Koblenz

- Description: Reach the city of Koblenz, where the Mosel meets the Rhine. Explore the Deutsches Eck (German Corner) and Ehrenbreitstein Fortress, immersing yourself in cultural and historical highlights at this junction.

Junction 7: Winningen

- Location: Winningen

- Description: Cycle through the charming town of Winningen, surrounded by vineyards and historic architecture. This junction offers a relaxing stretch along the scenic Mosel Valley.

Junction 8: Bernkastel-Kues (Again)

- Location: Bernkastel-Kues

- Description: Rediscover the medieval beauty of Bernkastel-Kues as you pass through once more. This junction provides a fresh perspective on the town, inviting you to explore its wonders again.

 Junction 9: Trittenheim

- Location: Trittenheim

- Description: Conclude your memorable Mosel Radweg journey in Trittenheim, embraced by vineyards. This junction marks the end of your cycling adventure and allows you to reflect on the diverse landscapes and cultural gems discovered along the Mosel River.

These key junctions not only serve as navigational markers but also provide opportunities for cyclists to immerse themselves in each unique location's character along the Mosel Radweg. Enjoy every moment of your journey as you pedal through history, vineyards, and charming towns.

Welcome to a list of some amazing hotels in Germany! Let's dive right in and explore these wonderful accommodations in different cities.

1. Trier's Porta Nigra

If you're visiting Trier, Germany, make sure to check out Hotel Deutscher Hof Trier. Located at Simeonstraße 1, this hotel offers a great experience. You can contact them at +49 651 97780 or visit their website [here](https://www.deutscher-hof-trier.de/).

Another option in Trier is Park Plaza Trier. Situated at Nikolaus-Koch-Platz 1, this hotel provides excellent service. Feel free to reach out to them at +49 651 99930 or visit their website [here](https://www.parkplaza.com/trier-hotel-de-54290/gertri).

---

2. Schweich

In Schweich, Germany, you can find Hotel Restaurant Zum Stern. Located at Brückenstraße 24, this hotel offers a delightful stay. You can contact them at +49 6502 93210 or visit their website [here](https://hotelzumstern.com/).

Another option in Schweich is Hotel Restaurant Ambiente situated at Brückenstraße 22. This hotel provides a cozy atmosphere and great amenities. Feel free to reach out to them at +49 6502 93720 or visit their website [here](https://www.hotel-ambiente-schweich.de/).

---

3. Bernkastel-Kues

If you're planning to visit Bernkastel-Kues, make sure to consider Hotel Moselpark Eventresort located in Im Kurpark. This hotel offers top-notch facilities and services for your enjoyment. You can contact them at +49 6531 9730 or visit their website [here](https://www.hotel-moselpark.de/).

Another option in Bernkastel-Kues is Wein- & Ferienhaus Hubertushof situated at Cusanusstraße 2. This charming hotel provides a cozy and relaxing atmosphere. Feel free to reach out to them at +49 6531 5215 or visit their website [here](https://www.hubertushof-bks.de/).

---

4. Traben-Trarbach

In Traben-Trarbach, Germany, you can find the Romantik Jugendstilhotel Bellevue located at An der Mosel 11. This hotel offers a romantic and elegant experience for its guests. You can contact them at +49 6541 8320 or visit their website [here](https://www.bellevue-hotel.de/).

Another option in Traben-Trarbach is Hotel Moselschlösschen situated at An der Mosel 11 as well. This hotel provides a luxurious and memorable stay with its stunning architecture and amenities. Feel free to reach out to them at +49 6541 8320 or visit their website [here](https://www.moselschloesschen.de/).

---

5. Cochem

Last but not least, if you're visiting Cochem, Germany, make sure to check out Hotel Karl Noss located at Moselpromenade 23. This hotel offers a picturesque view of the surroundings along with comfortable accommodations. You can contact them at +49 2671 2893 or visit their website [here](https://www.karl-noss.de/).
Another option in Cochem is Hotel am Hafen situated at Sehler Anlagen 15. This hotel provides a great location near the harbor and excellent hospitality. Feel free to reach out to them at +49 2671 9090 or visit their website [here](https://www.hotel-am-hafen-cochem.de/).

--

6. Koblenz - Deutsches Eck

If you're looking for a place to stay in Koblenz, Germany, you might want to consider the Mercure Hotel Koblenz. Located at Julius-Wegeler-Str. 6, this hotel offers comfortable accommodation and can be reached at +49 261 30390. You can find more information on their website: [Mercure Hotel Koblenz](https://all.accor.com/hotel/5366/index.en.shtml)
Another option in Koblenz is the GHOTEL hotel & living Koblenz. Situated at Neversstraße 15, this hotel provides a convenient location for travelers. You can contact them at +49 261 30370 or visit their website for more details: [GHOTEL hotel & living Koblenz](https://www.ghotel.de/)

---

7. Winningen

For those planning a trip to Winningen, Germany, the Hotel Nora Emmerich is worth considering. It is located at Moselstraße 52 and can be reached at +49 2606 377. To learn more about this hotel, you can visit their website: [Hotel Nora Emmerich](https://www.hotel-nora-emmerich.de/)

Another option in Winningen is the Hotel Weinstube Kesselstatt situated at Moselstraße 51. You can contact them at +49 2606 96340 or visit their website for further information: [Hotel Weinstube Kesselstatt](https://www.weinstube-kesselstatt.de/)

---

8. Trittenheim

In Trittenheim, Germany, one option for accommodations is the Burggasthaus Layensteig located at Römerstraße 9. To make a reservation or inquire about availability, you can call them at +49 6507 98350. For more details, you can visit their website: [Burggasthaus Layensteig](https://layensteig.de/)

Alternatively, you may consider the Weingut Gästehaus Hermann-Layenhof situated at Trittenheimer Straße 9. They can be reached at +49 6507 1550 and you can find more information on their website: [Weingut Gästehaus Hermann-Layenhof](https://www.layenhof.de/)

1. Komoot:

  - Platform: Available on iOS and Android devices.

  - Features include:

    - Turn-by-turn voice navigation to guide you along the route.

    - Offline maps for areas with weak or no signal.

    - Highlights points of interest along the way.

    - Allows you to record and share your cycling adventures.

  - For more information, visit the

[Komoot](https://www.komoot.com/) website.

2. Strava:

  - Platform: Compatible with both iOS and Android devices.

  - Key features include:

    - GPS tracking for accurate route navigation.

    - Records cycling metrics for performance analysis.

    - Community features for sharing routes and connecting with

fellow cyclists.

    - Special segments feature designed for competitive cyclists.

  - To learn more, check out [Strava](https://www.strava.com/)

website.

3. Google Maps:

  - Platform: Available on both iOS and Android devices.

  - Notable features include:

- Detailed maps with voice-guided navigation to help you stay on track.

- Real-time traffic updates and alternative routes to avoid congestion or delays.

- Offline maps that can be downloaded in advance for areas without internet access.

– Provides information about points of interest and local businesses along the way

– For more details, visit [Google Maps](https://www.google.com/maps) website.

4. Ride with GPS:

– Platform: Compatible with iOS and Android devices

– Key features include:

– Turn-by-turn voice navigation to guide you through your journey

– Offline maps available even in areas where there is no cell reception

– Elevation tracking feature helps in planning your route accordingly

– Route planning tools available on their website

– Learn more at [Ride with GPS](https://www.ridewithgps.com/) website.

5. Mapy.cz:

- Platform: Available on iOS and Android devices.

- Notable features include:

- Offline maps with detailed topography to ensure you have access to maps even without an internet connection.

- Voice-guided navigation for easy route following.

- Provides information about points of interest and services along the way.

- Elevation profiles available to help you plan your cycling journey effectively.

– For more information, visit [Mapy.cz](https://mapy.cz/) website.

6. Bikemap:

– Platform: Compatible with both iOS and Android devices

– Key features include:

– Cycling-specific maps designed specifically for planning routes.

– Voice navigation and offline maps so that you can navigate even when there is no internet connection available

– Community-driven platform where users can share their own routes

– Allows you to record cycling statistics to track your progress

– To find out more, visit [Bikemap](https://www.bikemap.net/) website.

7. Naviki:

- Platform: Available on both iOS and Android devices.

- Features include:

- Bike-friendly navigation system tailored for cyclists' needs.

- Points of interest specifically curated for cyclists along the route.

- Offline maps and navigation capabilities, ensuring a seamless experience even without an internet connection.

- Community features that allow users to share their routes with others in the cycling community.

For additional details, please visit [Naviki](https://www.naviki.org/) website.

Before embarking on your Mosel Radweg adventure, it is recommended that you download your preferred navigation app, make sure to have offline maps available in case of weak signal areas, and familiarize yourself with the unique features each app offers. Additionally, having a backup power source for your mobile device will come in handy during longer cycling days.

1. Trier Tourist Information:

   - Location: An der Porta Nigra, 54290 Trier, Germany.

   - Contact: +49 651 978080

   - Website: [Trier Tourist Information](https://www.trier-info.de/)

2. Bernkastel-Kues Tourist Information:

   - Location: Gestade 6, 54470 Bernkastel-Kues, Germany.

   - Contact: +49 6531 500190

   - Website: [Bernkastel-Kues Tourist

Information](https://www.bernkastel.de/)

3. Cochem Tourist Information:

   - Location: Endertplatz, 56812 Cochem, Germany.

   - Contact: +49 2671 60040

   - Website: [Cochem Tourist

Information](https://www.cochem.de/)

4. Koblenz Touristik:

   - Location: Zentralplatz, 56068 Koblenz, Germany.

   - Contact: +49 261 303880

   - Website: [Koblenz Touristik](https://www.koblenz-

touristik.de/)

5. Traben-Trarbach Tourist-Information:

   - Location: Brückenstraße 4, 56841 Traben-Trarbach, Germany.

   - Contact: +49

6541 83980

- Website: [Traben-Trarbach

Tourist-Information]

(https://www.traben-trarbach.de/)

6. Zell (Mosel)Tourismusinformation:

- Location : Balduinstraße 44, 56856 Zell (Mosel), Germany.

- Contact : +49 6542 96220

- Website: [Zell (Mosel) Tourist Information](https://www.zell-

mosel.com/)

7. Cycling Office Rheinland-Pfalz:

  - Location: Schubertstraße 10-18, 56075 Koblenz, Germany.

  - Contact: +49 261 9159970

  - Website: [Cycling Office Rheinland-

Pfalz](https://www.radwanderland.de/en/)

These tourist information centers offer valuable assistance to cyclists traveling along the Mosel Radweg. They provide maps, recommend accommodations, and share information about points of interest. Don't hesitate to visit these centers and make the most of your Mosel Radweg experience.

9 788819 683056